VANCOUVER

THEN & NOW

By ROLAND MORGAN

Whitecap Books
North Vancouver, B.C.

Copyright © Roland Morgan 1983
ISBN 0-920620-47-7
First Edition 1983

Published by
Whitecap Books Limited,
1086 West 3rd Street,
North Vancouver, B.C.
V7P 3J6

Printed in Canada

Introduction

Most of Vancouver's character architecture has survived by luck. It was pure luck that the business centre moved away from Main and Hastings, for instance, leaving the old warehouses to doze for a generation until their picturesque tourist potential was realized in time to save them from the wrecker's ball and create Gastown. The last of the blueblood mansions that once studded the West end, the Rogers residence, happened to be made of solid Gabriola stone and annexed to an apartment building, otherwise it would have been bulldozed under like hundreds of others. The clergy's plan to demolish Christ Church cathedral and join the skyscraper landlords was exposed by the press when it was well under way. The Canadian Pacific railway station was only saved from demolition by an economic slow-down and a new transit scheme. Hycroft, a grand lumberman's palace in Shaugnessy Heights that was left to the nation survives because the federal department of veteran's affairs decided to sell only half of the property to a private developer and the rest to a private club. The trees we call Stanley Park were earmarked early by federal military authorities. These are the survivors.

There were many casualties, such as the Edwardian C.P.R. station, the Pantages Theatre and the McLeery farm on the Fraser, which all went under unmourned. It was the crass vandalism of tearing down the Birks building, Vancouver's Georgia and Granville landmark, which finally triggered a measurable change of heart at city hall. The fight over that building and its totally unnecessary destruction made at least a few influential people aware that roots breed character and that character is priceless. The campaign of architecturalists like the University of British Columbia's Harold Kalman, or of lone activists like Stephen Brown, hounding the wrecking rectors of Christ Church, helped to show that all city planning seemed to protect was sewers and blacktop, and even blacktop it choked up with dangerous vehicle traffic.

It was time to re-assess. The quality of urban life could no longer be taken for granted: the 1960's had shown that engineering had the power to distort an environment into a profit-making machine that did wonders for balance sheets but caused havoc in terms of crime, health and housing. Arthur Erickson's provincial government building, commissioned by a new regime in Victoria, consciously abandoned the skyscraper ethic and left central open space behind Frank Rattenbury's courthouse building. High-density urban living on the European and Asian models became a desired goal.

That's where the past comes in. A look at the Hastings Street sidewalk eighty years ago, with mothers pushing strollers, Derby-hatted gents passing the time of day, bicycles racked on the kerb and non-polluting rapid transit rolling down the street illustrates a convivial lifestyle that is the ideal of today's enlightened architect. The mid-twentieth century city got stunned by the onslaught of high-speed elevators, automobiles and television, but the street is slowly making a come-back and the place of the past in the future is being recognized along with its heritage of inter-personal contact, variety and human scale. Ottawa's re-developement of a post-industrial Granville Island has shown the success of this trend.

It was a wild rush, 1886 to the first century, culminating in plans for a giant Expo. There were some lulls, a couple of world wars to be fought, but as the year 2000 approaches, the pace hasn't slackened. The archival treasures salted away by a born pack-rat named James Matthews, working out of a tiny office in a city hall annex, is beginning to look like something retrieved from an architectural dig. The contents of his bulging old filing cabinets and hand-me-down mayoral desk have been lodged in state under a piece of space-age architecture, getting more precious and curious every day — those pictures of ten-foot diameter spruces being felled where the Denman Place Inn now soars. . . the haunting portraits of aboriginal communities later obliterated in the rush for spoils. . . that record of the early individualists, each a caricature. . . the Edwardian city, oozing confidence and style.

But it is important not to let nostalgia warp the excitement of comparative photography. We love the human scale of the Edwardian city and rightly call it a flowering of modern urban living, however the stylish old towns, from Paris to San Francisco, hid fire hazards, ill-lit spaces, poor plumbing and disease behind their hand-crafted facades. Picturesque Chinatown was a racial ghetto and the milltown surrounded by burners often stank like hell. Nevertheless, there are things to be salvaged from the trail and comparative photography is one of them, more than a mere visual curiosity because each comparison projects an invisible picture that can only be imagined: the future one. What *will* this place be like in another hundred years?

Victorian boosters would have had a ready reply consisting of a rack of figures or a handy slogan, but these days the question makes people anxious. As *Time* put it a year or two ago: *The air is full of fear too large to grasp. Thus people turn to particularities they can deal with and at the same time accelerate their lives to get everything in before the fall.* Buildings get too big, jobs too bureaucratic, the tyranny and carnage of automobiles too universal. Then and now comparisons are startling measures of acceleration. They are also compulsive insights into collective origins for an immigrant population who have only the sense of place to unite them.

In 1983 as this exercise in comparative photography goes to press, the C.P.R. city has lived through an entire industrial era and emerged at the other end cheering on building projects as grandiose as any in its instant history: an enormous harbour pier, a huge downtown settlement, a 60,000-seat arena, a port-encircling highway and, ironically for a town which ripped up its extensive tramcar system, a 'light rapid transit' line and transport fair, the whole scheme still dogged by the social costs of a boom-and-bust economy. By any name, greed or glory, the motive hasn't changed since they hung banners over Hastings Street in 1905 blazing: *Many Men Making Money Means Much For Vancouver.* Chamber of Commerce rhetoric was never so pithy.

Acknowledgement goes to Vancouver Public Library and to Vancouver City Archives for permission to reproduce the archive pictures in this book. Twenty-three of them appeared in the 1978 edition; the rest have been freshly selected, and all the text and 'now' pictures are new.

INDEX

Historical photographs reprinted by permission of Vancouver Public Library (VPL) and Vancouver City Archives (CA). Contemporary photographs by the author.

THEN The waterfront from Stanley Park c. 1905
Bustled and befurbeloed ladies and men in 'Christie' stiff hats, Prince Albert coats and stovepipe trousers take the sun; prominent in their view is the Pacific Coast Lumber plant and burner (right). Coal Harbour was an industrial area. Parts of the park beach were residential (left). The granite structure at right was a horse trough. The first generation of apartment buildings can be seen going up on the skyline.

NOW **The waterfront from Stanley Park**
A seawall was built round the park as soon as the wash from heavy propellor-driven ships threatened to erode the shore. A de-industrialized Coal Harbour has been filled with pleasure craft and the CPR still dominates the beach with its 1971 32-storey tower (farthest left) built on the site of the only gulley in the low cliff bordering Burrard Inlet.

THEN North on Granville Street from Georgia 1906

Plank sidewalks and dirt road show the weakness of the tax base of the early company town. At far right is the second Hudson's Bay store, next to it is a private liquor store, the 1891 New York block and further down with a tower is the 1890 Bank of Montreal building. The 1898 CPR station, gateway to the rest of Canada, stands at the foot of the street. Traffic kept left until 1923. The building at left was called the Sons of England block.

NOW North on Granville Street from Georgia

As business kept moving eastwards the whole of Granville's east side was replaced by a new generation of commercial buildings. A third generation was launched on the west side in 1971, the mammoth Pacific Centre with its underground shopping centre; and a third generation development is slated for the half-block north of the Hudson's Bay store. Rapid transit remains partially electrified, but most of the rolling stock is decrepit.

THEN **North foot of Granville Street 1909**

    The Canadian Pacific Railway company's third station followed a pair of wooden waterfront buildings in 1898 and within ten years was too small for the flood of trade and immigration that came with the start of the new century. Designed in the Caledonian Chateau company style by Montreal architect Edward Maxwell, this nordic gem was one of the shortest-lived public buildings in history.

NOW North foot of Granville Street

The fourth station was built abutting the earlier one (if only it could have stayed that way!) in 1913; then the chateau was felled in 1914. The new station adopted the Beaux Arts classical style made fashionable for North American railway stations at the 1893 Chicago exhibition. It escaped planned demolition in the early 1970's, being restored in 1976 and linked to the Seabus and rapid transit system. The murals in the 150-foot long waiting room were painted in 1916 by the sister-in-law of the current company Superintendent.

THEN 1489 McRae 1927

This is Hycroft as it looked when occupied by the flamboyant Senator McRae, U.S.-born lumber baron and 1914-18 war Canadian forces general. Designed by Thomas Hooper in Italianate style, much of its building materials came from Italy for noble fireplaces, interior and roof tiles and travertine floor in the lower lounge. The palatial interior also featured a super de-luxe multi-directional shower in marble and chrome in the senator's bathroom. The landscaped garden included davidia trees and a mature sequoia (neither visible). On the right, just out of the picture, were extensive greenhouses, bowling alleys, a squash court and tennis courts with adjoining lounge.

NOW 1489 McRae

In 1942 the McRae family, unable to staff Hycroft during wartime, gave the house to the nation. It became a nursing home for armed forces veterans. In 1962 this public property was inexplicably sold to a private club: the University's Women's Club of Vancouver and this potential art gallery, seat of government or old-age home is used for exclusive needlework circles, charity bazaars and snob weddings — relatives of members only. The property was split with the sale and its recreational complex was torn down for condominiums.

THEN 1399 Johnston 1925

Granville Island was reclaimed by the federal government during World War One and leased to heavy industry. What had been a marshy bird sanctuary banged, clattered and belched smoke for sixty years as companies like Britannia Wire Rope raced to fell the fabulous virgin forests of the coastal mountain range.

NOW 1399 Johnston

By the 1970's heavy industry had no place in the city core and Granville Island was transformed into a post-industrial culture and commerce estate with the Emily Carr College of Art and Design (1980) as its focus. Following government policy, architects stayed within the 'Cannery Row' mode, echoing the style of the earlier factory buildings.

THEN Kitsilano Beach (then called Greer's Beach) 1908

This beach was first named after Sam Greer, who in the 1880's had a cottage on the site of the wooden boathouse (right). In the 1890's Greer's beach was a camp ground. Two rows of tents were established with a sandy lane between them. A herd of elk occupied a swamp in the forest beyond. The street car reached the beach in 1905 after the Canadian Pacific Railway had renamed the district Kitsilano in honour of Chief Khatsahlano of the Squamish Indian band. Sanitation of tent town became a problem in 1908 and in the following year the area was sub-divided by the C.P.R. for residential development.

NOW Kitsilano Beach

The topography of Kits beach has been altered by landfill and tidal action, taking the beach about 150 feet to the west. The swamp occupied by the herd of elk was filled with sand from the dredging of False Creek and five houses built by the C.P.R. to encourage settlement led to a Kitsilano population of more than 50,000, about half of them apartment dwellers. Sanitation problems still loom, with the beach occasionally being put out of bounds for bathing, but it remains one of the finest prospects on a sunny day, and one of the most dramatic in a storm.

THEN Water Street, looking S.W. 1909

Second generation brick and steel-frame commercial buildings stand beside earlier wooden structures like the Carter House (left) of 1886. Kelly-Douglas and Hudson's Bay had premises at the top right end of the street. David Spencer's new department store looms beyond. Note the numerous flagpoles ready for patriotic events.

13

NOW Water Street, looking S.W.
Woodward's parkade (left) was completed in 1971 after plans for massive demolition and re-building had been abandoned in the face of the Gastown rehabilitation campaign. The old commercial facades on the north side are completely intact. Spencer's 1928 addition and the 1976 Harbour Centre now dominate the end of the street. Well-intentioned trees actually obscure the picturesque facades in summer.

T HEN 640 West Hastings 1909

"One of the financial palaces of the Dominion . . . a Grecian monetary monument", the Vancouver *Province* gushed at the Canadian Imperial Bank of Commerce's completion in 1908. Actually, it was one of a series built using structural steel imported from Pittsburgh. Marble for the ornate interior was imported from France and Italy. Granite was brought from Kelly (Granite) Island to dress the exterior. The interior, a "veritable revelation" featured a vault claimed to be "cyclone proof and even proof against the shell of a warship". It was a symbol of the Canadian banking oligarchy for the upstart town.

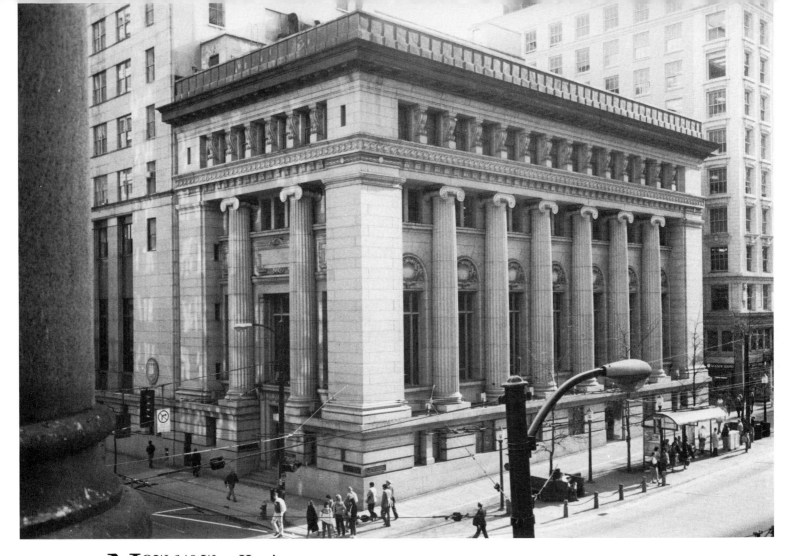

NOW 640 West Hastings

Glued to the new head office beside it, the Bank of Commerce temple remains externally intact, with the addition of some ground-floor windows, but the interior banking hall was entirely altered from 1951 to 1955 when the tower was being built, and was reopened in 1956 with lowered ceiling and most of the marble fittings stripped.

THEN foot of Chestnut Street 1895

Kitsilano Point was an Indian reservation that in 1942 was overrun by the city. Here Chief August Jack Khatsalano is shown in a dug-out canoe with his wife Swanamia. The boathouse on the beach is flotsam. Chief August Jack dug for his mother's gold on the beach in 1937. He died at a great age in 1967.

NOW Foot of Chestnut Street

The old beach was first reclaimed in 1913. Burrard Street bridge was built in 1932. The planetarium and Vancouver museum were built for the city in 1968 by lumber tycoon H.R. MacMillan. The inverted tea-cup and saucer design was a last-minute addition. The maritime museum (1958) was supplemented with the R.C.M.P. vessel St. Roch building in 1966. The whole was called the Vanier Park cultural centre.

THEN Foot of MacDonald 1941

The McLeery farm house overlooking the Fraser delta was the city's first pioneer residence, built in 1873 by Irish brothers Fitzgerald and Samuel McLeery. The pair were the first to farm the delta lands by dyking and draining, and the house was a community centre serving as hospital, school and church. It was one of the few buildings to survive the fire of 1886, a fire which McLeery watched in the sky from his garden.

NOW Foot of MacDonald

Tax troubles started to plague the McLeery family. In 1938 Fitzgerald's daughter had to fight for a grace period in which to collect her crops. Taxes on the farm had totalled about $100,000 since 1908. A tax court disallowed the plea, and by 1955 the house and property had to be turned over to the city, which in spite of some controversy proceeded to demolish the structurally sound residence and turn the farm into a golf course, a coric act of philistinism which caused archivist James Matthews to complain: "We can spend millions on a synthetic culture symbolized by the Canada Council, but we can't take the trouble to preserve a farm house whose antiquity represents the point where culture begins."

THEN Yew Street area 1890

The whole Vancouver townsite was prime timber stand. Yoked oxen yarded the felled trunks to a steam locomotive logging railway which carried them to English Bay at the foot of Trutch Street where they were dumped over a cliff onto Jericho beach. Boomed at the beach, the logs were towed to Hastings sawmill. The skid road consisted of greased logs. Oxen were yoked in teams from five to eight strong.

NOW **Yew Street**
A century later, the only echo of heavy logging on this Kitsilano slope of *sushi* bars, cut flowers and condominiums is in the street name itself.

THEN Burrard and Georgia Streets, Looking N.W. 1887

The Canadian Pacific Railway company was given nine square miles on which to build Vancouver. On freshly-cleared land they built solid stone and wood-frame 'cottages' like this one occupied by C.P.R. land commissioners until it was sold, enlarged and turned into the fashionable Glencoe Hotel. Under the impact of the economic crash the hotel was demolished (1932) and its furniture auctioned off.

NOW **Burrard and Georgia Streets, looking N.W.**
The Royal Centre was built on the site in 1971, a banking pavilion, 38-storey office tower, 720-room Hyatt hotel and 70-store underground shopping centre. In 1940 the site had been a parking lot.

A VANCOUVER HOME.

THEN 1523 Davie Street 1905

Sugar tycoon B.T. Rogers built himself "Gabriola" in 1901 when the West End was called Blueblood Alley for its ranks of expensive homes. The stone came from Gabriola Island and was put to best use in the multi-block style with tall chimneys and circular gazebo. The wood-panelled interiors had eighteen fireplaces. The spacious garden featured a greenhouse and Davie Street was a gracious boulevard, if a little muddy. Income tax was unknown.

ENTRANCE to
VALET PARKING →

NOW 1523 Davie Street

In 1924 "Gabriola" was annexed to an apartment building and called The Angus, which saved it from destruction until the Dominion Construction Company assembled the entire block with the intention of levelling everything on it. Finally the house was preserved as a restaurant, but its picturesque coach house and converted stables were demolished for condominium housing.

THEN Hastings and Richards Streets, looking E. 1905

Cycling was an integral part of city life at the turn of the century. The roadster at right incorporated pneumatic suspension in its rear fork assembly and carried a bell for warning the numerous pedestrians of the approach of the fastest vehicle on the street. The bike is resting in a rack, a convenience so rare now as to be almost extinct. Downtown was close enough to walk the baby down in a buggy on a sidewalk where besuited gents paused to pass the time of day. In this convivial ambience, the automobile was an object of ridicule.

NOW **Hastings and Richards Streets, looking S.E.**
Wonder of wonders, there is still a bicycle rack beneath the city's tallest structure, Sears' Harbour Centre, where the sidewalk has been extended beneath the building, a rare donation of extra space by a developer to the public.

THEN **The waterfront 1906**

The port of Vancouver in a boom era. The short city wharf is to the left, the rest is serviced by the C.P.R., headquartered in its 1898 chateau railway station. There were still no grain terminal elevators, or other rail and road system. Waterfront patrols were started in 1908 and three federal harbour commissioners were appointed in 1913.

NOW The waterfront

Heavy cargo traffic has left the city waterfront, although total trade through the port of Vancouver nearly doubled in the 1970's and is expected to continue to rise steeply with Asian demand for Canadian bulk resources, which form 85 per cent of exports. About 200,000 cruise ship visitors are the chief trade at the C.P.R. piers each year and the Seabus terminal has the busiest traffic. The two chief landmarks are the Harbour Centre (centre) and the C.P.R. tower (right).

THEN 355 Burrard Street 1944

No expense was spared on Vancouver's finest office block, the Marine Building, by its Toronto developers in the heady economic climate of 1929. Vancouver architects McCarter and Nairne described it as "some giant crag rising from the sea, clinging with sea flora and fauna, tinted in sea green and touched with gold." After the crash the city council refused to buy it for one million dollars and it went to a Guinness family company for $800,000 in 1933. A superb three-storey penthouse contains a small Czechoslovakian chandelier that cost $8,500 in 1930. The workmanship of the portico and concourse are rightly treasured.

NOW *355* **Burrard Street**

 Still Guinness-owned, the Marine Building is in good condition with many of its original tenants, and now under renovation. To its left, a ten-storey customs building was raised in 1954 and beside it is a 32-storey office tower, part of the Bentall Centre begun in 1965.

THEN **Hastings and Abbott Streets, looking N.W. 1907**
Charles Woodward opened his second Vancouver Premises in 1904, after launching on Main Street. In this boom era of full employment and mass immigration Woodward's in the east and Spencer's in the west bounded the central business district.

NOW Hastings and Abbott Streets, looking N.W.
 The building had a fifth storey added in 1908, a new wing in 1914, a self-serve food floor of advanced design in 1919, an extension to Cordova in 1925 and an extra storey in 1929 with a tunnel under Cordova to a parking garage. A ten-storey section was added in 1948, and a ramp to a 900-car garage in 1956. After that expansion spread into other cities and other provinces. The food floor is still a popular attraction.

THEN **Prospect Point, looking N. 1902**

The light and signal station at Prospect Point were installed in 1874. Mariners were greeted by the wreckage of the S.S. Beaver (left), a pioneer Hudson's Bay steamer which worked Oregon when that territory was British, finally sinking as a tugboat in 1888. The Capilano Indian village is visible across First Narrows.

NOW Prospect Point

Nobody wanted the First Narrows bridge except the developers of north shore properties. Mariners opposed it; the federal government feared the competition against its own Second Narrows bridge; and a Vancouver plebiscite in the 1920's rejected the associated highway through precious Stanley Park. But during the 1930's economic crash the job prospects made another plebiscite successful and the 1550-foot span was opened in 1938, charging tolls until the province acquired it in 1956. Re-decking began in 1975, but the volume of traffic causes heavy wear and tear and there are frequent casualties.

THEN 'Granville' 1880

The Indians' 'Lucklucky', or beautiful grove, was named Granville by the handful of European settlers who worked at the Hastings sawmill near New Brighton beach. They called Water Street Front Street and looked out on freshly-felled spruce stumps. The balconied building at the centre was the 1872 Granville Hotel, where mail was distributed. To its left was the customs house where the first council meeting of the city of Vancouver was held in 1886, just before the whole village burned down. The CPR railhead arrived in 1887.

NOW 'Gastown'

The picturesque facades of Gastown owe their survival to the departure of the business centre westward. The area was rehabilitated in the 1970's and named after bar-operator 'Gassy Jack' Deighton, a Granville pioneer.

THEN 43 Powell Street 1912

Designed by local architects Parr and Fee, the Hotel Europe was the first reinforced concrete structure built in Vancouver and the first fire-proof hotel in the Canadian west. The framework was built by contractors from far-away Cincinnati, the nearest experts. The design imitated the 1903 New York 'flatiron' building and its lobby was a marvel of functional marble and brass.

NOW **43 Powell Street**
This Gastown gem survives with a few modifications. Its main entrance was blocked off to create a lavatory for the beer parlour and the lamps on the entrance balcony got lost. Long threatened with 'demolition by neglect', the hotel is under renovation.

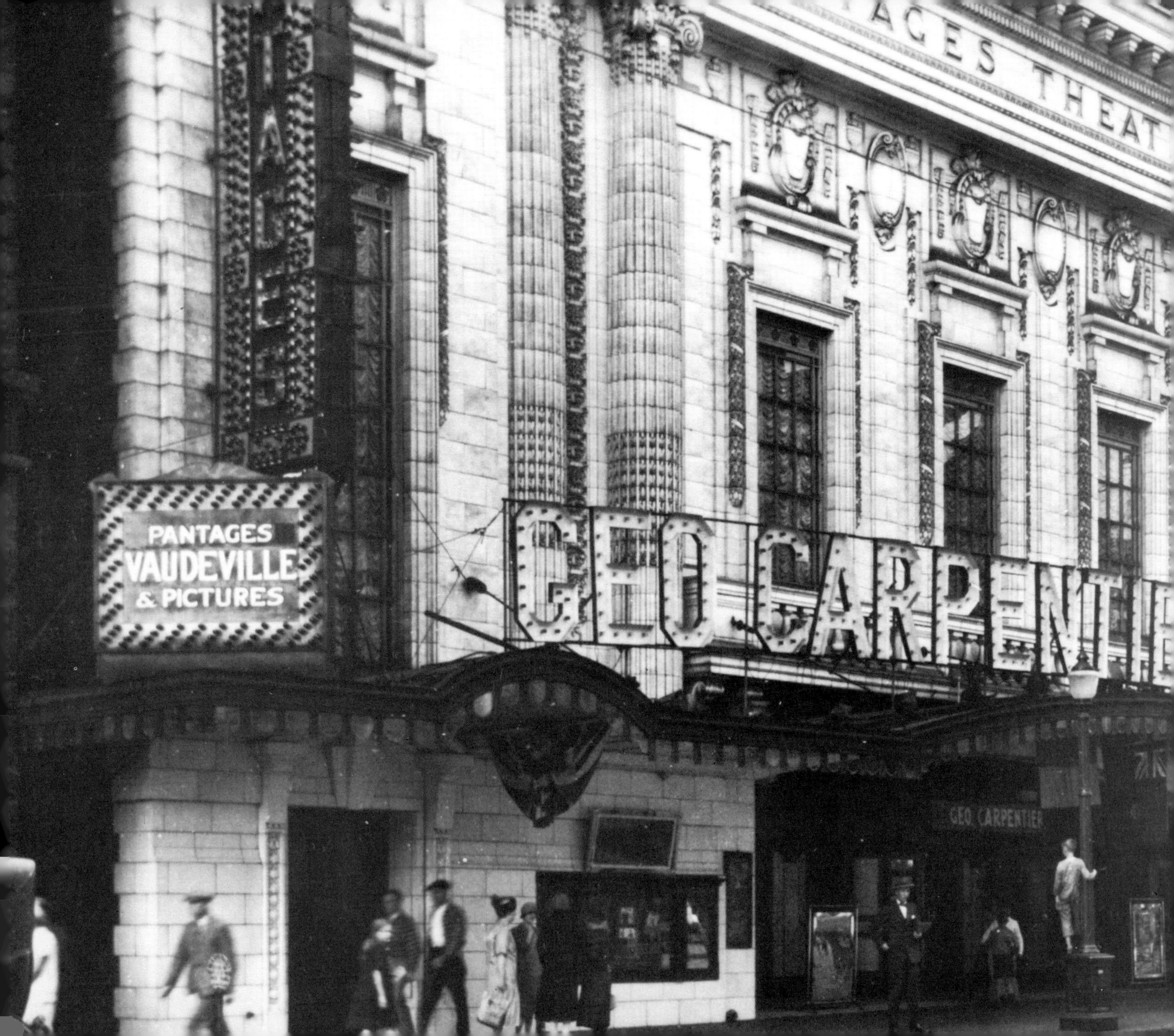
PANTAGES
VAUDEVILLE
& PICTURES
GEO. CARPENTIER

THEN 4 West Hastings Street 1925

Western theatre magnate Alex Pantages built his Vancouver theatre on West Hastings in 1917, next to the Cohen family's Army and Navy store and opposite another busy theatre, the Rex. The elaborate classical facade evoked Roman and Greek drama.

NOW 4 West Hastings Street

The Pantages went through seven re-modellings, still offering live legitimate theatre into the 1950's (hounded by police chief Walter Mulligan for obscenity). Its last incarnation, as the Majestic, started in 1958 and ended in 1964 when a parking company bought it and reduced a showbiz monument to rubble for a few dozen parking spaces.

THEN Panorama, English Bay 1938

After the wealthy had fled the West End across the new Granville Street bridge to install themselves in Shaugnessy Heights, the peninsula remained a hodge-podge of converted homes and three-storey walk-up apartments dominated by the eight-storey Sylvia Hotel (formerly apartments). The population in 1938 was about 25,000.

NOW Panorama, English Bay

The West End apartment boom started in 1960 and ended in 1972. Zoning regulations allowed 380 persons per acre, five times as many people as live there now, present density being seventy-seven persons per acre, lower than Manhattan (100 per acre) or St. Jamestown district in Toronto. The resultant scheme of isolated towers is now considered a success and is to be the model for west False Creek settlement.

THEN **Hastings and Carrall Streets, looking west 1932**
C.P.R. locomotive 252 makes one of its last shunting trips to False Creek before the street crossing was abandoned in favour of a tunnel. The old B.C. Electric streetcar building (left, 1912) would soon be turned from a bus station into a bank branch. The Rex Theatre (beyond the loco cab) started in 1912 in a converted Bank of Montreal building and until its closure was the longest-operating cinema in the west. Note the Buscombe building on its left (see next layout).

NOW **Hastings and Carrall Streets, looking W.**
Removal of the C.P.R. spurline led to establishment of Pioneer Place (far right) outside the 1913 Merchants Bank building, a sunning spot known as Pigeon Park to locals.

THEN 27 West Hastings c. 1908

The mayor of Vancouver and chairman of just about everything else, Fred Buscombe, built this airy, contemporary store for his British imports business. Edwardian marketing strategy did not forbid customers to look out of windows. A Richardsonian Bank of Montreal branch stood next door, gracefully arched and pilastered in brick.

NOW 27 West Hastings
The Buscombe
building, later Cal-Van
Market, was sold in 1938 to
the east-side discount house
Army & Navy stores, who
later removed the cornice,
blocked the windows and
modified the ground floor
facade. The Bank of
Montreal building lived on
as the Rex cinema from 1912
to 1959 when it was
demolished to make way for
a store extension.

THEN **Hornby and Robson Streets, looking N.E. 1919**

Frank Rattenbury's neo-classical revival courthouse of 1906 almost immediately needed a rear wing addition, which was built in 1912 (centre left). The 1914 second Hotel Vancouver, with its pergola'd roof garden, was overlooked only by the clock of the 1910 Vancouver Block beyond. The concrete chimney served a laundry located in the hotel annex at its foot. To the south were residential blocks.

NOW **Hornby and Robson Streets, looking N.E.**
Two chartered bank towers rear up behind the 1970 Eaton's store, half a million square feet of selling space with practically no windows. Robson Square, a community centre, is buried under the street and covered with landscaping. The courthouse lives on, adapted into a municipal art gallery.

THEN Granville Street, looking north from Georgia 1905

Paved sidewalks were slowly making their appearance in Vancouver during the boom immigration era, particularly outside such establishments as the Hudson's Bay store (right). Only infants dared appear in the street hatless.

NOW Granville Street, looking north from Georgia

Life at Granville and Georgia is now conducted on two levels, since the invasion of Eastern underground arcade merchants in the 1970's. Underground transit stations threaten to drive a large part of downtown life completely underground by 1986. This trend was not subjected to any kind of public referendum, but imposed by financial muscle in spite of Vancouver's temperate climate.

THEN Panorama, south shore of False Creek 1926

Vancouver spent most of its first century as a milltown ringed with smoke stacks. False Creek was a watery industrial backyard where the forest plunder was brought to be processed for export. Girth of the logs in the boom at right shows how plentiful first-stand timber was, only half a century ago.

53

NOW **Panorama, south shore of False Creek**
The south-east shore now boasts swanky condominium housing and marina space for luxury pleasure craft. Such settlements are populated by the swelling ranks of middle-class professional and bureaucrats in the million-plus city. Log booms are still to be seen, but not for long, once the huge schemes for the west shore are completed.

Many Men Making Money MEANS MUCH FOR VANCOUVER

THEN West Hastings Street, 400-block looking W. 1905

The second generation of commercial buildings were all walk-ups, and personal transport was chiefly on foot, which has led some social critics to blame the elevator and the automobile for the modern passion for fitness: Edwardians were forced to stay fit just by getting around. Much energy was expended on boosterism, too. Other west coast ports were competing vigorously for Pacific trade. The distant banners read "Hurrah! Tell Our Tale! Talk Our Town!" and "Vancouver 100,000 in 1910". At left is the city's first 'temple' bank, the 1903 Royal Bank head office. Under the word 'Making' is the McMillan building, Vancouver's first stone post office.

NOW West Hastings Street, 400-block looking W.

NA third generation of buildings replaced the Edwardian facades, beginning with the Standard Building (centre left) which at fifteen storeys in 1913 made it the city's highest single-slab building. The Royal Bank's 1931 tower (centre right) is visible beyond the 1928 portion of the block-sized Harbour Centre. The 1930 Marine Building dominates the end of the street.

THEN *555 West Hastings Street 1927*

Welsh merchant David Spencer, established in Victoria, launched a new store in Vancouver in 1906 in the building under the coat of arms. By 1927 his emporium had engulfed the Italianate Molson's Bank (1898) building at the end of the block, the Bank of Toronto next to it, and a nine-storey addition had been built on the east end, the last word in excellence in its day, decorated with sculptures in art-stone. Spencer later occupied the superb penthouse at the peak of the nearby Marine Building, whence he could survey his empire. The decorations celebrate the nation's half-century.

NOW 555 West Hastings Street

The Edwardian buildings were demolished in 1973 to make way for the 35-storey Harbour Centre, whose height and revolving restaurant feature were subject to much jockeying in the corridors of city hall. The 455-foot high restaurant is now a familiar landmark on the skyline.

THEN **Squamish Indian village 1888**
   The Indian fishing village founded by French monks (Oblate order) in 1867 was for twenty years bigger than fledgling Granville on the opposite shore, and was said to rival any European settlement. The church seen here was built by the inhabitants in 1884. The Oblates also founded Sechelt mission village. By 1900 the work of the monks was being eroded by industrialization, disease and the language barrier.

NOW Squamish Indian village

The tideflats have been filled in and the B.C. Railway passes in front of the twin-spired church built on the foundations of the earlier church in 1909 to a vernacular design by Oblate Father Petrayvin. Urban development now has this settlement, which was jealously guarded by the monks against encroaching whites or unconverted natives for forty years, stategically positioned on priceless property.

THEN Stanley Park 1897

Stanley Park owed its existence to the U.S. military threat of the 1860's, when the point was made a military reserve for target practice and ship's spars. Townspeople first crossed Lost Lagoon on a tree trunk and some boulders. Later the first park rangers built a plank bridge and stick arch. The ranger's cottage is visible beyond the bridge. There was no access to the lawns at Brockton Point from the nearby streetcar terminal. Intrepid British aristocrat Lord Stanley dedicated the park in 1889. For many years, no traffic was allowed in the park between two and five p.m. on Saturdays and Sundays.

NOW Stanley Park

A seawall and perimeter drive was created in the 1920's and the park was bisected by a highway in 1937 which threatens to create one of the city's toughest traffic headaches when inevitable high-density development occurs on empty blocks bounding the park entrance. The mighty tree preserved at the foot of Georgia (visible at left in 1897) was felled for roadworks in 1920.

THEN **364 Water Street 1892**
The Holland Block was designed by an unknown architect in the San Francisco style with big bay windows which both captured light and created extra floor space. The building adjoining it (centre right) was for twenty years the premises of the Red Cross brewery. Beyond it is the picturesque Horne Block, a Victorian Italianate edifice with cupola and Juliet balcony built in 1889.

NOW 364 Water Street

Alas, the Holland Block was unsympathetically modified during the depression years, losing its rounded cornice and biggest bay windows, but it was not subjected to the radical stripping suffered by the Horne Block, which lost all its fussy sculptured ornamentation.

THEN **West Georgia Street at Richards, looking W. 1927**
 The Hudsons Bay store (centre right) had been completed in 1925. The Strand theatre opposite it (1919) was part of the Allen chain of Ontario, which later formed part of Famous Players. A car showroom in California Spanish style was under construction at the time of this royal visit. The rear of the Birks building (centre left) lacked terracotta facing.

NOW **West Georgia Street at Richards, looking W.**
Only the Hudson's Bay store survives, designated a heritage building by city hall. The Strand was demolished in 1975 to make way for the 34-storey Bank of Nova Scotia tower. Beyond it is the Toronto Dominion bank tower and right of centre the 18-storey International Business Machine tower. The Spanish-style showrooms were felled for a car park building.

THEN Granville and Robson Streets, looking S.W. 1891

The Opera House was part of the grand plan for Vancouver's original townsite conceived and executed by the Canadian Pacific Railway. The company surveyed the forest into streets, named them after its executive, cleared the timber and started building. They built Pacific steamships, the first Hotel Vancouver, then the Opera House, in that order. The opera was constructed in 1890 at 765 Granville, behind the first Hotel Vancouver, and the first performance was *Carmen* on February 9th, 1891. The ornate interior featured a fire-screen painted with a landscape of the Three Sisters at Banff, Alberta. New owners painted this over with advertisements almost immediately. The Opera House became successively the New Orpheum, Vancouver Theatre, Lyric and Cinema until its demolition to make way for Eatons' department store in 1968 (inset)

THEN **Panorama of Vancouver N.W. 1904**

Howe, Hornby, Burrard and Hastings Streets were entirely residential. These were the first of the C.P.R.'s residential lots. Right centre is the Badminton Hotel with the Vancouver Club at far right. Squatters' homes were visible on the beaches of Stanley Park. North and West Vancouver are partially logged-off forest. This shot was taken from the Hotel Vancouver.

NOW **Panorama of Vancouver N.W.**
In the foreground is the Georgia Hotel; to the left is the Georgia Medical-Dental building, under threat of demolition; beyond it the Four Seasons Hotel, the Bentall Centre, the 35-storey Park Place under construction, the Marine Building in the distance and at far right a Howe Street office block.

THEN **Howe and Dunsmuir Streets S.W. 1892**
    The Manor House hotel stood on quiet, residential Howe Street for forty-seven years, known for most of its life as the Badminton. It illustrates some of the benefits of doing without elevators: a guest on one of the balconies can talk to someone on the street, for example — and there's plenty of sky left for everyone. At top left is an electric-arc street light, its carbon renewed daily.

NOW **Howe and Dunsmuir Streets S.W.**
Business activity soon spread up Howe
Street from the waterfront. The 1978 office
building at 625 Howe shows the trend towards
smaller-scale business towers, but it also illustrates
how elevators and air-conditioning divorce
modern architecture from the street.

THEN 900-block West Hastings Street, looking N.E. 1927

The Vancouver Club tore down its wood and brick mansion in 1912 to replace it with a gentlemens' club worthy of St. James's in London. Behind the Georgian revival exterior, designed by select London architects, is a luxurious interior featuring a harbour-view dining room panelled in imported Austrian oak. The 1926 Seaboard House (centre left) housed shipping offices.

NOW 900-block West
Hastings Street,
looking N.E.

Daon Developments, a
continent-wide property developer,
chose this site, strategically located
at the entrance to the federal
government's harbour pier
complex, for their 19-storey
corporate headquarters. The $20
million building is faced with gold-
filled reflector glass imported from
South Africa which at the right time
of day gives a fine image of the
Marine Building opposite. Daon
was later reported in trouble with a
billion-dollar debt burden.

THEN West Pender and Cambie Streets, looking E. 1920

An Edwardian commercial gem, the 1912 Sun Tower was built by publisher and Vancouver mayor L.D. Taylor for his Vancouver *World* newspaper which had to move out in 1915. The Vancouver *Sun* occupied the premises between 1937 and 1964, serving its production shop a block away by motorcycle couriers.

NOW **West Pender and Cambie Streets, looking E.**
Designated a heritage building, the main office block is in good repair, but the tower, complete with its cupola and 'Jules Verne' mansard windows, is threatened with 'demolition by neglect'. The site is once again strategic as False Creek re-development approaches beyond.

THEN Panorama of False Creek, looking N. 1911

The C.P.R.'s Fairview subdivision overlooked the railway's shunting yards on the north side of False Creek. Churches were mariners' landmarks on the skyline, from the Wesleyan at Georgia and Burrard (centre left) to the Methodist, Presbyterian and Catholic (centre left).

NOW **Panorama of False Creek, looking N.**
Fairview became a mixed-use area until city hall designated it part of the False Creek re-
development plan and property costs rocketed with smart condominium housing developments. False
Creek started to fill up with pleasure craft and its north shore lies cleared, ready for installation of
Expo '86 pavilions and further housing and commercial re-development to create a completely de-
industrialized False Creek. The 1983 B.C. Place stadium is a new landmark at the right.

THEN English Bay 1904

West Indian pioneer Joe Fortes settled English Bay after discovering it on a rowing trip in 1884. It was cut off from Granville village by thick forest. By 1893 there was a 'two-plank road' via Robson and Denman Streets and a short-cut footpath through the forest. The veteran of British windjammers became an Edwardian celebrity, acting as lifeguard at English Bay beach every summer for twenty years until his death in 1922. Properties on the beach were already being bought by the city between 1902 and 1911, and the ramshackle beach facilities shown here were replaced by a pier and a more substantial building in 1909. The rocks were cleared in 1905.

79

Now English Bay
The Promenade area was built in 1931, replacing a wooden beach building, and sand has been dredged onto the beach several times, extending it into the sea. The 1912 Sylvia Apartments, now the hotel, once dominated the foreshore, but the population of the West end highrises alone now equals that of the entire city in 1905.

THEN 800-block Granville Street 1929
Seattle architect Marcus Priteca designed
the Orpheum in 1926 for a Chicago-based
vaudeville chain. The 2,800-seat craftsman-
built auditorium and multi-level foyer made it
one of the biggest theatres on the west coast.
The Granville Street facade was only a foyer
leading to the theatre building behind on
Seymour. As the canopy shows, live acts were
mixed with silent cinema.

NOW 800-block Granville Street
The Orpheum's interior was threatened when big cinemas no longer paid and a multiscreen complex was planned, but by popular demand and subscription the auditorium and foyer were restored to form a permanent home for the Vancouver Symphony Orchestra. The project became a landmark restoration job, with the original artist supervising. The theatre was re-opened half a century after its construction, in 1977. Only the sign scaffolding remained little improved.

THEN **North Vancouver waterfront c. 1870**
   The first ship departed from Colonel Moody's sawmill for Adelaide on November 9th, 1864. Employees' housing (centre left) was the first European settlement on Burrard Inlet, and home of the first Vancouver area newspaper, the Moodyville *Tickler*, founded in 1878. Hand-logging was straight-forward: fell the trees and roll the logs into the sea.

NOW North Vancouver waterfront

The post-modern framework exterior of the 1981 Insurance Corporation of British Columbia headquarters was the first building in a commercial, educational and residential complex being launched on the waterfront at Moodyville by the British Columbia Development Corporation. Beyond the I.C.B.C. buildings is Burrard dry dock with a ferry boat under repair. One of the Seabus shuttle vessels enters the North Vancouver terminal.

THEN Cordova Street at Carrall, looking W. 1905

Cordova Street was Vancouver's business centre in the 1890's. Activity moved onto Hastings and westwards during the 1900's, never to return. At left is the Lonsdale Block of 1889, the longest frontage of its day, once holding many prime businesses as well as Vancouver's Reading Room. The Boulder Hotel (far right) contrasted rusticated masonry with plain windows in un-Victorian simplicity. The streetcars were part of the biggest network in Canada, reaching sixty miles up the Fraser valley to Chilliwack.

NOW **Cordova Street at Carrall, looking W.**
The Boulder Hotel received a third storey addition in 1910. The Lonsdale Block facade is kept in good repair by a department store which gutted the rear of the building for an annex. In the distance, Woodwards Stores installed a pedestrian ramp to serve their parking building in 1956. The streetcar system was dismantled after World War Two with the advent of mass automobile ownership.

THEN 850 West Hastings Street 1946
The Credit Foncier building, Vancouver
head office of a Montreal-based mortgage
company, was built in 1914, one of Vancouver's
third generation of commercial buildings. An
early elevator-served building, its scale is
impressive without being daunting, a quality
architects are seeking once more in the 1980's
with moderately-sized office towers.

NOW 850 West Hastings Street
As befits the premises of a mortgage company, the Credit Foncier building has been well maintained over an uneventful life, and in 1974 its concrete frame construction with cut-stone sheathing exterior in a neo-classical mode were designated for heritage protection status.

THEN The Waterfront from the foot of Main, looking W. 1886

Newly-named Vancouver in its founding year, arising out of the ashes of its disastrous fire, the Canadian Pacific railhead still at Port Moody but on its way to Coal Harbour, communications with Vancouver being served by the navigation company's sidewheeler Princess Louise, which is seen here calling at the city wharf near the foot of Main Street. In the distance, beyond the former Granville townsite, the C.P.R.'s nine square miles of government-ceded land are being cleared, leaving the military tree reserve which became Stanley Park in the distance. In the foreground are railway sleepers cut for the advancing line. Hastings Sawmill is out of sight to the right.

NOW **The waterfront from the foot of Main, looking W.**
Landfill was extended hundreds of feet into Burrard Inlet to accomodate the railway yards and port-associated industry. With de-industrialization of the downtown area the foreshore has been cleared and is temporarily used for police force parking. In this view the C.P.R. tower looks particularly prominent in its prime position commanding the waterfront.

THEN West Hastings Street at Granville, looking E. 1905

This picture shows some of the picturesque second generation commercial facades which were once not confined only to 'Gastown'. The tallest building with heavy cornice is Davis Chambers, a legal building of 1906. Beyond it (with arches) is the Richardsonian Empire Building, one of Vancouver's oldest blocks, built in 1888 around an internal courtyard with a funky open-cage elevator. The next building is Molson's Bank of 1898. In the foreground is Trorey's jewellers, later bought by Birk's, who moved the clock to Georgia and Granville Streets. People walk freely on the street, even in their freshly-laundered best (right).

NOW West Hastings Street at Granville, looking E.

The ponderous Royal Bank tower was built on this block in 1931, just before the economic depression of the 1930's. The Davis Chambers building was demolished in 1977 to make way for an undistinguished office building and the Empire Building was turned into a hole in 1979, awaiting its replacement.

THEN Georgia and Granville Streets, looking S.W. 1934

The second Hotel Vancouver was an Edwardian marvel with gracefully arched windows, generous setback with *porte cochere* and a vast roof garden with vine-draped pergola. It started operation as a Canadian Pacific Hotel in 1914, just in time for the First World War and ended its life as a billet for Second World War troops. The hotel's name was transferred to the C.N.R.-C.P.R. joint venture replacement on Georgia at Burrard on its completion in 1939.

NOW Georgia and Granville Streets, looking S.W.

The thirty-storey Toronto Dominion bank tower and monolithic Eatons department store were built as part of a massive 1969 Eastern-financed development comprising this block and the block to the north of it. The tower was instantly dubbed the Black Tower by a disenchanted public which found the concourse beneath it uncomfortably draughty, a phenomenon caused by large monolithic buildings. However the developers countered complaints by inviting shoppers to enjoy the day underground in their shopping centre or in the half-million square feet of windowless store-space beyond the cylindrical stairwell.

THEN **Western business district panorama, looking S.E. 1933**
    This photograph, taken from the newly-completed Marine Building, shows the between-wars downtown area as it would largely remain until the new impetus of the 1960's. At right, the massive Hotel Vancouver, started in 1928, was still unfinished and would remain so until 1939, when the C.N.R. and C.P.R. would operate jointly under its distinctive green copper roof. The hotel whose name it would assume (centre) stood a relic for ten years until it was demolished in 1949. At the foot of the new hotel is the 1889 Christ Church cathedral.

NOW Western business district panorama, looking S.E.
The twin black towers (centre left and far left) of the early 1970's Pacific Centre now dominate the western core. The 35-storey Park Place rises between them and the wall of towers on the west side of Burrard Street, leaving the cathedral dwarfed on its strategic corner site, the survivor of a 1973 demolition scheme—now protected by heritage status.

THEN **Stanley Park, view of Brockton Point 1925**

The site where this photograph was taken from was once a Squamish village, Whoi-whoi, and seafood shells from middens made by Coast Salish Indians were used to pave the first paths in Stanley Park, a thousand-acre patch of practically untouched forest which was saved by a mid-century military threat from the U.S.A. The lighthouse and foghorn at Brockton Point were established in 1890.

NOW **Stanley Park, view of Brockton Point**

A seawall was built round the park during World War One to protect the beaches from the wash of ocean-going freighters as they entered the port of Vancouver. The perimeter road was formed at the same time and paved during the 1920's, following the exact routing proposed for it at the end of the nineteenth century by the C.P.R. land commission . Here, at Lumberman's Arch, the road ran right through a historic midden and many skeletons were revealed, buried by inhabitants of a village which had been emptied by the ravages of smallpox.

THEN Main and Hastings Streets, looking S.W. 1900

From 1896 to 1929 Vancouver city hall was located in the Market Hall, built in 1889 for auctioning cattle and poultry and the staging of public events. In this view the auctioneer is still next door. Previously city hall was on Powell Street. When South Vancouver and Point Grey municipalities amalgamated in 1929, a temporary city hall was located in the Holden Building at 16 East Hastings, until the imposing new city hall on 12th Avenue was opened in 1936. Meanwhile, the city had turned down an opportunity to buy the Marine Building at the foot of Burrard Street, now one of Canada's architectural treasures.

NOW **Main and Hastings Streets, looking S.W.**
The Carnegie Library on the corner was completed in 1903, one of scores of such libraries founded by U.S. industrial magnate Andrew Carnegie. It served as a public library and civic museum until 1968, the old city hall serving as an annex until its demolition in 1958. The library decayed until 1976 when the city finally decided to renovate and install its departments of health and social services there.

THEN Coal Harbour, looking N.W. 1921

Coal Harbour used to be a log pond for a lumber mill. Vancouver arena is visible at the left, housing the city ice rink, and on the far shore the city rowing club (centre) and Royal Vancouver Yacht Club (right) can be seen. In the foreground, shipbuilding yards and C.P.R. rail lines.

NOW **Coal Harbour, looking N.W.**
Extensive landfilling reduced the size of Coal Harbour and created a prime site
for the Bayshore Hotel, built there in 1960 with a tower addition in 1969. Pleasure
craft filled the remaining water space, creating a post-industrial tourist and recreation spot.

THEN View from Cambie Bridge, looking N.W. 1904

The first Cambie Bridge cost $12,000 in 1891 and was just wide enough for two wagons to pass. Made entirely of wood on piles, it had a draw span which in early days was opened about once a year. It was paid for by a south False Creek sawmill to save the long hard haul round the creek for their horse-drawn lumber wagons. The Vancouver skyline was punctuated with a rank of now-demolished churches.

NOW **View from Cambie Bridge, looking N.W.**

Turning the camera just a little, we find Vancouver's newest and biggest landmark, the 1983 B.C. Place Stadium, with pneumatic roof awning and dry seats for 60,000. Before it had been opened, parking was already a controversial question. The 1912 Connaught Bridge, an important traffic feeder, was also controversial because of huge re-settlement plans for the downtown False Creek area. The bridge crosses the site of the city's 1986 Exposition.

THEN 470 Granville 1922

A fine monument from Vancouver's 1908-12 boom period was the typically Edwardian Rogers Building, located on a prime site just yards away from the Canadian Pacific rail terminal. Built in 1911, it was named after Jonathon Rogers, a builder and land speculator, to the design of Seattle architects Gould and Champney.

NOW 470 Granville

This elegant and assertive structure is still structurally sound, its neo-classical terracotta exterior and marble and hardwood decorated interior lending grace and character to the foot of modern Granville Street; designated a Heritage Building in 1974.

THEN **Robson and Jervis Streets, looking S.W. 1930**
  J. M. Dent, the publishing house, chose this dignified private home for its Western Canadian office, managed for years by Gordon Stephen, literateur and epicurean, amidst oak-panelled rooms with blazing hearths. Many West coast authors frequented this residence over the years. The publisher occupied the ground floor of 'Aldine House' and the United Nations Association was upstairs.

NOW **Robson and Jervis Streets, looking S.W.**
Dents' gracious way of conducting business came to an end with skyrocketing West End property values, and the site of Aldine House is now occupied by a late 1960's motel built in the International style.

THEN Foot of Main Street, looking N. 1888
The brand-new single-track C.P.R. railhead passes in the foreground, crossing the entrance to Hastings lumber mill, Vancouver's founding industry. Six sailing ships are seen loading lumber. At the centre of the picture is the Hastings Store, which was later removed to Jerry's Cove where it serves as a folk museum.

NOW Foot of Main Street, looking N.
The site of the mill today is a nondescript industrial wharfage area, with the C.P.R. tracks multiplied to three.

THEN Burnaby Street, looking N.E. 1905

The company town's tax-free elite settled the West End, occupying grand residences, but with the construction of the new Granville Street bridge in 1909 these people started to move to the C.P.R.'s exclusive Shaugnessy Heights subdivision, leaving their big houses to be converted into rooms and apartments. Sidewalk paving has begun here on the south side, but the north side remains a boardwalk. Twenty years earlier this had been virgin forest.

NOW Burnaby Street, looking N.E.

Housing patterns here have entirely altered to a population consisting mostly of the elderly and childless couples, with what planners call '1.4 persons per dwelling unit'. But mobility is lower than commonly believed in this high-rise district: about sixty per cent of residents have occupied their place for five years.

THEN Georgia and Granville Streets, looking N.E. 1908

The Bay's second Vancouver store led the trend to the west by establishing at Georgia and Granville in 1893 when Cordova and Hastings were the chief business areas. In its new location (it had been launched on Water Street) the store was handy for Blueblood Alley in the West End and for Hotel Vancouver guests. When further space was required, the first section of the new store building was built adjoining this one to the right in 1913 and for twelve years parts of the old store still served, until the whole building had been replaced.

NOW Georgia and Granville Streets, looking N.E.
Completed in 1926, the current store building was the fifth outlet built by the pioneer company in Vancouver in forty years. The H.B.C. had founded the first settlement in the Fraser Valley at Fort Langley in 1827, 167 years after it was royally chartered in London to conduct the North American fur trade. The balustrades along the top of the building are of plywood. The cream terra cotta Corinthian columns were once a company trademark. This was declared a Heritage Building in the wake of the destruction of the historic Birks building opposite.

THEN **Burrard Inlet ferry service 1908**
A ship called the S.S. North Vancouver was placed in service in 1900, fare ten cents to downtown Vancouver, to be replaced within a few years by the vessel shown here, the Saint George, which ended life destroyed by fire after serving as a floating bunkhouse. The ferry system had its finest hour during the Second World War fuel rationing, carrying seven million passengers in 1943. The fifth ferry vessel made its last crossing in 1958, axed because of a required $100,000 subsidy.

NOW Burrard Inlet ferry service
The North Vancouver ferry took nineteen years to recover from the impact of the car, yet bicycles are still allowed on the new Seabus service only on Sundays and holidays. The trip takes only eight minutes in one of the modernistic ferry vessels, which are equipped with escape hatches in the floor leading to chutes out of the side of the hull. The service will be integrated with Greater Vancouver's new rail transit system.

THEN Carrall Street at Pender, looking N.W. 1906

Chinese immigrants built the Canadian Pacific railway line through the Rockies, then were consigned to a ghetto south of the city core. This row of buildings, some of them with typical Chinese recessed balconies on the upper storeys, hid Shanghai and Canton Alleys, where poor rooming houses were mixed with a red light district and opium factories.

NOW **Carrall Street at Pender, looking N.W.**
Racial prejudice caused a clamp-down on Chinese immigration in the inter-war years, leading to the de-population of Chinatown's western extemity. Only a brutally modified 1903 Chinese Empire Reform Association building (centre) and the 1901 Chinese Freemason's Building (right) survive on the fringe of an otherwise re-vitalized Chinatown.

THEN Robson and Thurlow Streets, looking N.E. 1912

Lumber magnate W.L. Tait owned a fine residence on this site, but he could spot a trend and had his house demolished in 1907 to construct the Manhattan Apartments, one of the West End's first residential blocks. It was designed with fashionable bay windows by local architects Parr and Fee, designers of the 1910 Vancouver Block visible in the distance (far right), giving each apartment a room with a view. The building's success led to an addition which is under construction at the right. There was an airy tea garden on the roof. Tait moved to Shaugnessy Heights, where he built 'Glen Brae', now a listed heritage building.

NOW Robson and Thurlow Streets, looking N.E.

The Manhattan Apartments were saved from demolition in 1980 by their incorporation into a co-operative housing association which with low-cost loans conducted a handsome renovation and re-created an enviable address on miraculously low-rise Robson Street.

THEN Panorama, looking W. 1935

At far left are the Ritz Apartments; the Sylvia Apartments are visible in the distance on English Bay; and the Park Plaza Apartments are just right of centre. These were the big buildings of the inter-war era, when the West End was a mixed residential area. Photo taken from the top of the new Marine Building.

NOW Panorama, looking W.

The two towers of the Bentall Centre are at left, with the honeycomb MacMillan Bloedel building beyond them, the Canada Trust tower to the right, with the two-tone 1050 West Pender and one of the Guiness towers in the foreground. Beyond, the West End is hodge-podge of hotel towers and apartment racks.

THEN Georgia and Granville
Streets, looking S.E. 1925

The Birks building became a bit of an institution after its construction in 1912. People met by the clock, often under its metal sidewalk canopy out of the rain. The craftsmanship in its elaborate terracotta facade became unrepeatable with the disappearance of old crafts after World War One. The building was made even more attractive by the ill-proportioned 1910 Vancouver Block next door (it had an attractive roof terrace.) The Strand theatre (far left) was built in 1919.

NOW Georgia and Granville Streets, looking S.E.

The destruction of the Birks building in 1975 caused a furore in the city and a feud even in the Birks family itself. In city hall there was a year-long minority attempt to revoke planning permission; opponents of destruction argued that the existing building was compatible with offices scheduled to be built beside it. In the end the Montreal developers got everything they applied for. The replacement Birks store has a roof terrace which is seldom visited, and the clumsy Vancouver Block was declared a heritage building.

THEN Nicola and Alberni Streets 1889

Oben's skid road with a five-ox team, hand-logging the site of Vancouver a century ago, within the feasible life-span of a person. Here roamed bear, cougar, elk and moose, with a salmon leaping in the ponds.

NOW Nicola and Alberni Streets

The headquarters of an insurance company, Crown Life Place, was built in 1976 where Mr. Oben felled his spruce. *"Surely it is amazing that a city this size should come into existence in the lifetime of one man?"*

126

"Goodbye, Devonshire Hotel!"

About the author
Born in Brighton, England and educated at
Cambridge University, Roland Morgan has been
a university teacher, photojournalist, government
research officer, newspaper editor and book
publisher. He has composed *Then And Now* books
about San Francisco, Seattle, Honolulu, Victoria
and British Columbia and a historical album
called *Toronto the Good* (with Gerald Utting).